Project Plans To Build for Children

Edited by: Jean E. Attebury

Baby Articles	2
Toys For Fun	10
Rocking Toys	12
Toys On Wheels	16
Puzzles	22
Toys	25
Doll Accessories	29
Toy Boxes	36
Wooden Toys	42
Bedroom Accessories	50
Beds And Bunks	66
Useful Furniture	90
Outdoor Play	106
Ordering Information	126

In addition to the instructions and diagrams for many projects included in this book, complete plans, instruction details and materials lists are available for most projects. Order forms for these plans are included for your convenience.

Order Blanks	127

From the pages of

Better Homes and Gardens®

LEARNING GAMES FOR BABIES

Encouraging babies to explore their environments can be lots of fun for parents and also help the infant to develop his senses and motor skills. In addition to playing with the baby, parents should talk to him even though he cannot understand the meanings of the words. These conversations serve to help the baby learn to imitate language as well as giving him information about the feelings of the people around him.

1. Placing a shiny mobile above the crib, playing with a musical rattle, or stringing brightly colored balls across the crib will encourage the baby to focus and to reach for the objects.

2. Visual stimulation encouraging the baby to increase his field of vision can be accomplished by dangling a bright toy about 8 to 10″ in front of the baby at eye level. While moving the object back and forth, say "See, see," or "Look, look." Smile and voice approval as the baby tracks the toy with his eyes.

3. During bath time name the parts of the baby's body as you wash them. This will offer the opportunity for conversation as well as providing an atmosphere of familiarity with the procedure of bathing.

4. Although hands and feet are generally the preferred playthings during this period of development, provide brightly colored cloths, noisy toys, things to bite and suck that can be washed or cleaned easily.

5. Playing "I see you" will encourage the baby to raise his head while lying on his stomach. Crouch below the level of the bed on which he is lying and slowly rise while calling his name.

6. Place rattles or similar playthings in the hand. Although the baby may not hold onto it very long, his grasp will increase and he will eventually be able to hold it without dropping it.

All babies develop at different rates as the central nervous system is able to control the muscles. Although little change may be seen from day to day, these simple play activities will stimulate coordination and provide important communication and interaction between the baby and his parents.

1 CRADLE: Shown in mahogany, this beautiful cradle is $26 \times 43 \times 28''$. Destined to become a family heirloom, it will be treasured for generations to come. Plan #50436

2 CRADLE: This simple cradle is made of 3/4″ maple, has a $32 \times 16''$ base; bonnet is 28″ high. Plan #50270

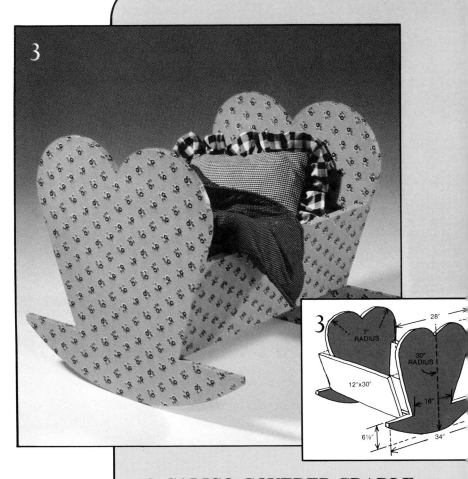

3 CALICO-COVERED CRADLE: Rock-a-bye your baby in one of the most appealing cradles around. Cut the 2 heart-shaped endpieces according to the diagram. Adjust the diameter of the curve using a pencil attached to a string. Next cut the 16″ bottom. Glue and nail the ends to it. Measure for the sides, and install them the same way. Then fill and sand the plywood edges. Apply calico fabric one section at a time, cutting the material to fit as you go. Apply spray adhesive to the wood, then press the precut fabric in place. Add a tiny mattress and pillow, and tuck in your little one.

4 SLING CRADLE: Double the pattern and transfer to plywood. Cut a 18 × 30″ piece of plywood for mattress support; cut eleven 19½″ pieces of 1″ wood dowel. Clamp sides together, mark positions of dowels, and drill a 1″ hole at each position. Unclamp sides; glue 9 dowels in place. Glue and nail mattress support. Upholster a 27 × 18 × 4″ foam mattress pad. For sling, finish the edges of an 18″ wide length of fabric. Position in cradle as shown. Fold ends under at each sling end; insert other dowels in casings to hold in place.

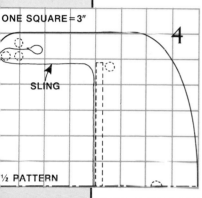

ONE SQUARE = 3″

SLING

4

½ PATTERN

5 CONTEMPORARY CRADLE: Rock your youngest to sleep in this clean-cut cradle. It's sure to become a family treasure that will be handed down from one generation to the next.
Plan #50403

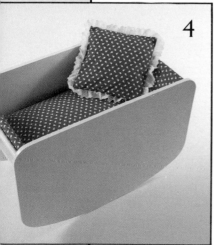

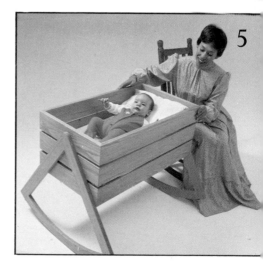

6 SWINGING CRIB: This standard-size crib goes together very simply and should take less than an afternoon. Cut 3/4″ plywood 30 × 541/2″ and nail frame of 2 × 2s on the underside. For the top rail, build another equal-size frame from 2 × 2s. Cut 1 × 2s for the mid-rails to the 541/2″ length. Stack these parts carefully, and drill 1/2″ holes (spaced every 31/2″) through all the pieces at once. This way, you'll ensure perfect lineup. Cut 1/2″ dowels to 29″ and inset them into the bottom, then force the mid-rails into position and the top rails on ends. Nail through the railings into each dowel. Cut an opening for the gate — it's made with 1 × 2s and dowels. Hang the crib by looping 1/4″ rope through screw eyes in the ceiling and tie at the base. Adjust the crib then wrap tape just below the ceiling bolts to prevent tipping.

7 CONTEMPORARY CRIB: A bright-eyed baby deserves something new to bed down in — and here it is. This handsome crib of plywood and pine is complete with a view, thanks to acrylic ends. The position shown is for an infant. Later on, lower the mattress and add longer acrylic ends. Plan #50308

8 HIGH CHAIR: Our classic wood high chair has a detachable tray you can remove when your child grows older. The chair stands 31″ high and measures 16 × 16″ at the base. You can make the chair from 3/4″ pine and birch dowels. We applied clear polyurethane varnish as a protective finish. Plan #50249

8

9 CRIB/CHANGING TABLE: Here's a crib that grows with baby to become a junior bed that will please any pre-schooler. For the infant there's a cozy crib plus a roomy changing table that takes up very little room in any small nursery. When it's time to move out of the crib, rearranging a few of the components produces a handy junior bed. Plan #50487

10 RADIATOR CHANGING TABLE:

What better place for changing the baby than over a radiator? Build the top and sides with 3/4″ plywood and use 1/2″ for the shelves. Size according to the space you have and allow an adequate opening for heat transfer. Make a simple frame the size of the opening, then glue on triangular wood strips to make a grille. Install magnetic catches in the corners to hold it in place. Attach the unit to wall or floor for extra stability.

11 NURSERY MIRROR: Extra storage

concealed within this nursery mirror is out of the way but easily accessible for changing. Plan #50325

LEARN AT HOME

There are plenty of simple ways for parents to help their children learn basic concepts and basic skills at home. The experts at the Home and School Institute helped Better Homes and Gardens devise a list of entertaining and educational projects which can be used throughout the year. These enriching activities can take a few minutes or a few hours. They require only a little of your supervision time and some inexpensive materials, most of which can be found around the house.

'Round-the-house reading and writing

1. Word train. Make a paper word train to post on a wall. Add a new car to the train for each new word learned. Color-code the cars. Words beginning with A can be red; B, blue; and so on.

2. Cut-up comics. Cut apart individual panels from comic strips and have children arrange them in logical order. Then come up with original dialogue for the comic strip characters.

3. Young authors. Use four white sheets of letter-size paper folded in half and stapled together. Cover with colored construction paper. Preschool children draw pictures and have adults do the writing as the children dictate. Elementary schoolers both illustrate and write their stories.

4. Photo stories. Clip photographs from papers or magazines. Pool them and take turns inventing stories, written or oral, using the photos to illustrate.

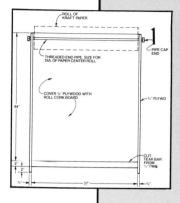

ROLL OF
KRAFT PAPER

B

1

PIPE CAP
END

THREADED END PIPE, SIZE FOR
DIA OF PAPER CENTER ROLL

COVER ⅜" PLYWOOD WITH
ROLL CORK BOARD

⅜" PLYWD

44"

CUT
TEAR BAR
FROM
¾" PINE

2"
2"
⅜"

37"

⅜"

1

1 NO MESS ART:

Begin by cutting two 16½ × 46" uprights from ¾" plywood. Measure 9½" from left to right along top edge and mark. From this point draw a line to the lower right-hand corner. Cut along this line to form a sloped front edge. Repeat. Cut a 25 × 46" piece of ⅜" plywood for the back, and a 25 × 2" piece of ¾" plywood for the tear bar. Center and drill a 1" hole 2" down and 5¼" from the rear edge on each upright. Draw lines on both sides of the hole at widest edge to top edge of upright; cut along these lines. Glue and nail plywood back between uprights. Cover front surface of back with thin adhesive cork. Nail tear bar near bottom between uprights, allowing ⅛" clearance between tear bar and back. Have a 27" pipe threaded and capped. Paint unit and pipe. Thread pipe through center of butcher paper roll and suspend in top grooves of uprights. Thread paper behind tear bar.

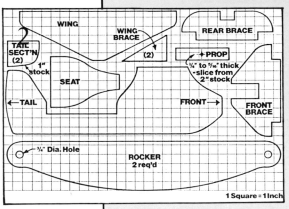

TAIL SECT'N (2)

1" stock

WING

WING BRACE (2)

SEAT

← TAIL

REAR BRACE

← PROP
¼" to ⁵⁄₁₆" thick slice from 2" stock

FRONT →

FRONT BRACE

¾" Dia. Hole

ROCKER 2 req'd

1 Square = 1 Inch

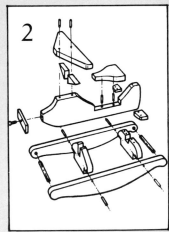

2 ROCKING AIRPLANE: For this virtually indestructible plane you'll need 13" of 2 × 8" pine; scraps of 1" pine; ³⁄₈" dowel, 33" long, for front and back stabilizers; glue; sandpaper; stain; varnish. Cut and assemble following the diagrams.

3 ELEPHANT ROCKER: Toss a throw rug on the back of this sturdy pachyderm so your child can rock comfortably through the nursery jungle. Plan #50444

4 NURSERY RHYME ROCKER: Remember the cow that jumped over the moon, while the dish ran away with the spoon? Our rocking version of Bossy will delight the younger set. Make the rocker seat double width if you what it to accommodate two youngsters at a time. Plan #50408

5 SWINGING AIRPLANE: Any young pilot can bank, dive, and climb in this plane that swings from a sturdy tree branch. It's cut from plywood, then sanded and painted. Nylon rope is threaded through pulleys at strategic points.
Plan #50183

6 ROCKING HORSE: A child's first independent excursion is likely to be astride a gentle steed in the nursery. To make those first rides truly memorable, build your youngster a rocking horse like this one, smooth of form and clean of line.
Plan #50328

7 SWAN ROCKER: You don't have to take your youngsters to the Boston Commons for a swan ride. Just build them this swan rocker for two from one 4 × 8 sheet of ³/₄″ AB exterior plywood.
Plan #50425

8 PAINTED ROCKING HORSE: This heirloom-quality rocking horse is a safe, sturdy toy. You can build it with basic workshop tools, then use a paintbrush for folk art flourishes.
Plan #50472

8

1 COASTER WAGON: Coaster wagons are great for hauling kid-size cargo. This ³/₄″ pine wagon is a generous 18 × 30 × 15″. The 8″ wheels are mounted on ¹/₂″ steel axles and the front wheels swivel on a metal lazy Susan.
Plan #50246

2 FARM WAGON: "Westward ho the wagon!" Ours is a child-sized version of the familiar corn-picking wagons of yesteryear.
Plan #50441

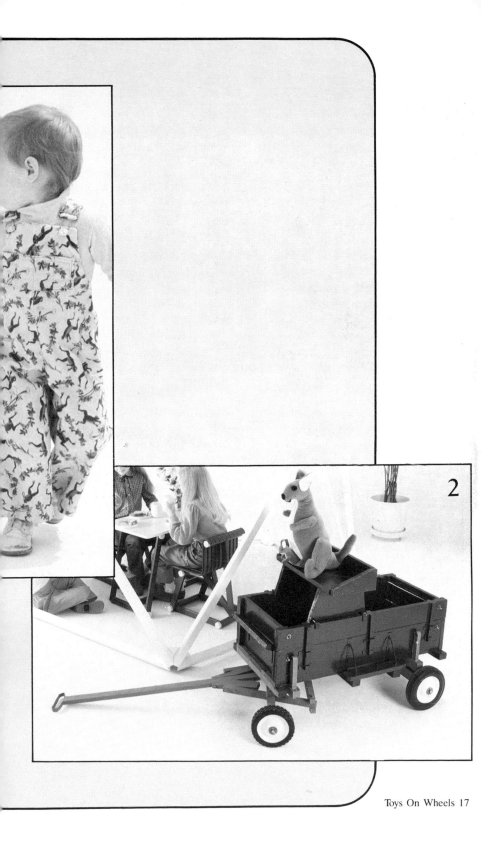

2

3 WOODBURNED PULL TOYS:

These old fashioned pull toys are cut from 2″ thick pine following the patterns after they have been enlarged to an appropriate size. After sanding the edges, cut four 2½″ wheels and a 3½″ wide base from ¾″ pine matching length to the decorative stand for each animal. Transfer the motifs and then woodburn them as desired. To assemble, drill ⅜″ hole through base for 5¼″ dowel axle. Drill ¼″ holes through wheel centers. Glue and nail base to bottom of animal. Insert dowels through base and glue wheels onto dowel ends. Varnish lightly after painting desired design. Pattern #01271

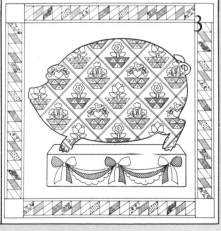

4

4 KIDDIE CAR: This nifty little number is sure to please all junior car buffs. It's built of sturdy plywood and mounted on metal casters so it can move easily over carpet or concrete for fun indoors and out. The lift-open trunk has lots of space for presents just waiting to be delivered. In the spring the driver can roll back the quilted top and soak up the sunshine. Plan #50344

5 KIDDIE TRUCK: Tots will haul other things besides puppies in this sturdy truck. The body is ³/₄″ plywood with 1 × 1s and 1 × 2s for the trim and bumpers. The wheels are fake; the truck actually rolls on 2″ rubber casters. Plan #50389

1 NUMBER PUZZLE:
Help toddlers learn their first numbers. Knobs atop each digit correspond to the number. Two pieces of plywood and paint are all you need.

2 CRECHE PUZZLE:
Here's an interpretation of the Nativity scene that's as simple and beautiful as the Christmas story itself. Completely made of clear pine, these figures are as exquisite as many more elaborate creche pieces. Plan #50330

3 PICTURE PUZZLES: Puzzles from your child's favorite pictures are easily made by gluing the pictures to plywood, cutting irregular pieces with a jig saw, then adding a protective coating of polyurethane.

4 STRATEGY PUZZLES: Wire and wood, lengths of cord and leather, plus a little paint — that's all you need to create these strategy puzzles. Test your persistence and problem-solving skills on the Dinghy and the Dock, the Christmas Tree, the Metal Maze, the Peppermint Twist and the Heart Teaser. Plan #50352

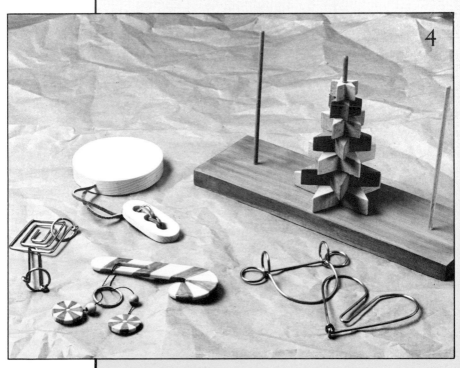

1

2

1 WALKING TRICYCLE: With a walking tricycle, who needs pedals? And without them, the trike is easier for you to build since the only moving parts are wheels and the handlebar joint. The joint swivels on a dowel in the center; disks cut from a vinyl floor tile protect it from wear. The 6″ rubber-tired wheels are mounted on 1/2″ steel axles. Aluminum tubing keeps the rear axle centered. Plan #50250

2 WHEELBARROW: Watch a youngster play, and you'll see that much of the time he's hard at work. To encourage that natural industriousness, build him a sturdy, child-size wheelbarrow so he can move mountains of sand or haul big block loads with ease. Plan #50271

3 SLED: This authentic-looking child's sled is simple to construct and will open the eyes of children and adults alike upon first sight. Recreate some of your fondest memories and inspire some for a child. Plan #50439

4 SNAIL CHALKBOARD: Cut a friendly snail or any other animal from a sheet of 1/4″ hardboard; then brush on green chalkboard paint.

5 FRIENDLY NIGHT LIGHT: What child wouldn't like to have this friendly 42″ bird standing watch at bedtime? The two sides of the bird are cut from 1/4″ hardboard. Blocks of 3/4″ plywood hold the wings away from the body so light can filter through. The 3/4″ tubing legs fit into plywood blocks that support the porcelain socket. The wiring runs through one of the tube legs and into the 12 x 12″ base made from 2 × 2s and 3/4″ plywood. The bright orange feet are made of 1/8″ hardboard.

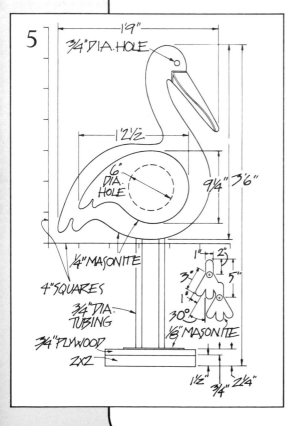

4

5

1 DOLL FURNITURE: Patterned after the furniture in George Rogers Clark's home, Locust Grove, this doll-size bed and chest will delight any young lady and be treasured for many years to come. Plan #50437

2 DAVE ASHE DOLL FURNITURE: What little girl could resist this "heirloom" Early American furniture for the dolls at her very own homestead? The doll-sized dry sink, hutch, cradle, and settle pictured are all made from pine. Plan #50373

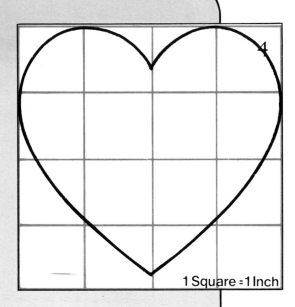

1 Square = 1 Inch

3 BASKET DOLL BED: Your cost on this project will be determined by the basket's size. Cut a piece of scrap plywood to fit in the bottom of the basket; screw through the plywood into half-inch-thick rockers. Add a cushiony "mattress," a pillow, and bedcovers and the doll cradle is ready for many sweet dreams.

4 HEART DOLL CRADLE: For this heart-shaped doll cradle you'll need ½ sheet of ³⁄₈″ fir plywood; #7 brass roundhead screws; medium grade sandpaper; natural finish Danish oil; wood glue; small nails. Enlarge the pattern and cut 2 pattern pieces from plywood. Cut two 5 × 16″ pieces for the 2 sides and one 5³⁄₄ × 16″ piece for the bottom. Sand all edges. Glue and nail the sides to the bottom, beveling the edges. Attach the 2 endpieces by gluing and nailing the pieces in place. After the glue has thoroughly dried, use 5 brass roundhead screws at each end to help secure the ends to the sides and bottom. Finish with a coat of Danish oil then add a tiny mattress and pillow.

5 DOLL CHEST: This miniature chest of drawers is ideal for storing all of those delicate doll clothes. Scaled to doll-size it will be treasured for many years after the dolls are put away for other toys. Plan #50440

6 CABINET DOLL'S HOUSE: What can
you do with a run-of-the-mill unfinished cabinet?
Turn it into a wondrous dollhouse. Just cut away
the windows and door, add a roof, and paint. Now
you have a dream house for your little ones or a
unique decorative cupboard for your best collectibles.

7 DOLL HOUSE: Help that budding interior designer with a miniature Better Home. You can assemble it in a few evenings, yet its basic construction is sturdy enough to last through several designers' lifetimes. Access is through the roof so there's a complete view of each room's floor plan. Add furniture and the chimney that doubles as a handle and this home will provide hours of enjoyment. To get inside, just lift off the peaked roof. Slotted walls and movable partitions make it possible to rearrange the interior instantly; there are dozens of different floor-plan combinations. Make the nineteen pieces of furniture from lumber scraps and bits of hardboard, then give each of them a quick squirt of paint from an aerosol can. Saw kirfs, staples, brads, and tacks serve as hardware and other details. The chimney doubles as a handle, so when it's time to put the house away, it can be used as a portable toy chest. It measures 25" long, 18½" wide, and 15" high, including the chimney-handle. Plan #50168

1 KIDS' FINANCE CENTER: Build these units with double-thick corrugated board as shown here or upgrade them with particle board. Each unit is $5 \times 3 \times 2$ feet; cut deep notches in each panel with a saber saw and just slip the panels together. Add dowels and an extra shelf for the bank. Lettering is press-on type.

2

Center

1 Square = 1 Inch

2 TOY BOX/PUPPET

STAGE: Unit serves double-duty and is constructed of one $4 \times 5\frac{1}{2}'$ sheet of $\frac{3}{4}''$ plywood. First build a box that's 18″ deep, 24″ wide, and 24″ high. While building the box, fashion a 21″ door across the back and mount on hinges. Leave the top of the box open, EXCEPT insert a 6″ wide strip of wood in the top and across the front of the box for the stage floor. The stage front is $18 \times 24''$ with the opening cut out. Transfer the enlarged pattern, paint as desired, add a curtain rod and it's showtime.

3 OUTDOOR TRAIN: Hitch up your garden tractor to these railroad cars which are simply plywood boxes with wheels and appropriate paint jobs. Build each car as you have time and you'll eventually have your own railroad. Plan #50086

4 RIVERBOAT TOY BOX: Our sturdy stern-wheeler is 36″ long, including the moving paddle wheel, and rolls easily on casters. The hinged lid can double as a toy storage chest. Plan #50247

5 HAND CARVED TOYS: You need not be
a master carver to create these primitive animal
toys. Cut simple animal shapes from weathered
pine or rough-cut lumber using a saber or band
saw. Use dowels as legs and shape with a coarse
file or rasp. Paint with a rag or sponge to achieve
the unique finish and add facial details and trim.
Use fringed leather for the horse's mane and tail
and small pieces for the ears. Drill holes in platforms of rough board for the legs and for the
wheels which may be made of wooden checkers or
slices of wooden broom handles. Use wooden
toothpicks and glue to attach the wheels to the
platforms.

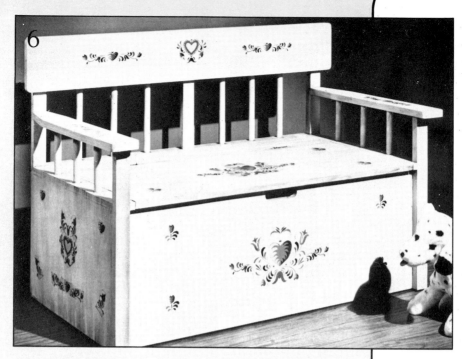

6 TOY CHEST: Build this child-size copy of an Early American boot bench to use as a toy chest in any room in the house. Only 14″ high with hidden casters, it's easy to roll around when it's time to straighten up after a day of play. Plan #50127

7 TOY BOX TRUCK: The 36 × 16 × 16″ trailer of this rig holds a heap of toys and other treasures. To personalize the 18-wheeler, paint the owner's name on the side. Plan #50434

8 COW TOY BOX: Our smiling brown cow is so appealing that your youngsters are bound to be more cooperative about putting their toys away. This sturdy bovine chest is 18 × 18 × 24″. Plan #50252

1 WOODEN TOYS: This sturdy steam engine is made from scraps of unfinished pine — as is the old-time biplane. The "man with four faces" stands in front of a mirror so you can see what happens when you spin his head.

Friendly Mr. Snake wiggles every which way with just a flick of the finger. Youthful imagination is all that's needed to take our horseless carriage for a spin. And Mrs. Busybody? She's quite agreeable to being jiggled around the room with her arms and dress in motion. Plan #50253

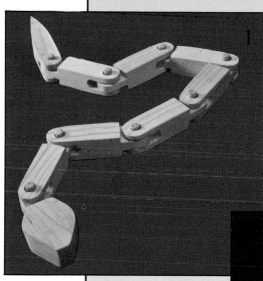

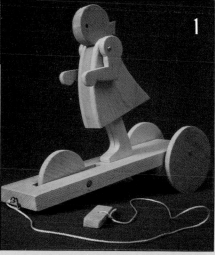

2 MOVING WOODEN TOYS: These action toys are reminiscent of Christmas Past and will be passed on to the next generation in some Christmas Future. Select a different toy each year until you've completed the entire collection. Plan #50228

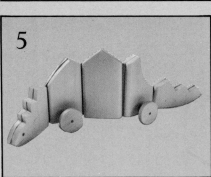

4

4

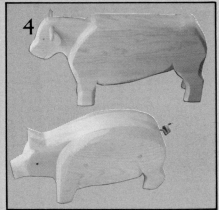

5

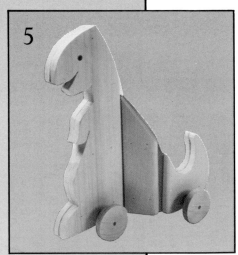

5

4 WOODEN TOYS AND MORE: From scraps of pine you can build these farmyard friends to delight your favorite children. Add the boat and the wagon and they'll be off into realms of fancy. Plan #50413

5 DINOSAURS: Cut these fanciful dinosaurs from scrap ³/₄″ pine; leather is used to hinge the sections. Join sides with brads at small dots; insert ¹/₄″ dowels at large dots for the axles; then attach 1″ circular spacers and wheels to dowels.

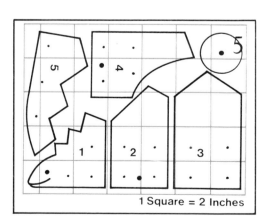

1 Square = 2 Inches

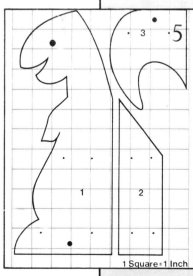

1 Square = 1 Inch

6 ACTION TOYS: It's a toss up who will get the most pleasure from watching these ingenious toys do their things — you or your youngsters. Not one of the toys needs batteries or electrical power,

yet all move, swing or spin with the greatest of ease. Each toy operates according to a basic mechanical principle so your children will learn while they watch. Plan #50329

Sorting Out and Counting Up Activities

1. Measure up. How tall is the lamp? How long is the room? Use rulers, yardsticks, tape rulers, string — anything that can measure. Measure in metric as well as inches, feet and yards. Record results of measuring expeditions on paper to share with others or use them for your remodeling projects.

2. Catalog shopping spree. With an imaginary $25 to spend, browse through some mail-order catalogs to select a shopping list of items. Keep a running total to be sure of staying within the limit.

3. Egg carton counter. Salvage an egg carton and write numbers in the bottom of each section. Add small scraps of cloth or paper to match the number in each section of the egg carton — two for the 2 section, three for the 3 section, and so on. Or, toss pennies or small buttons into the carton with the same objective.

4. Napkin fractions. Paper napkins can be folded into lots of big and little fractions. Start with halves and progress to eighths or sixteenths. Use markers to label the fractional parts.

5. Telephonitis. Combine reading and math skills by looking up the telephone numbers of friends and relatives in the directory. Then add up the total of the digits next to the names. You might also have each child make a personal phone book with numbers and addresses of people he's found in the big directory.

6. Liquid learning. Partly fill the tub or sink with water and add some plastic containers of various sizes — cup, pint, quart and gallon. How many pints in a quart? How many quarts in a gallon? It's not necessary to memorize all the measures — just explore the concepts.

1 CORNER TEEPEE: Built into the corner of any child's bedroom, this tee-pee will lead to hours of imaginative play. Plan #50324

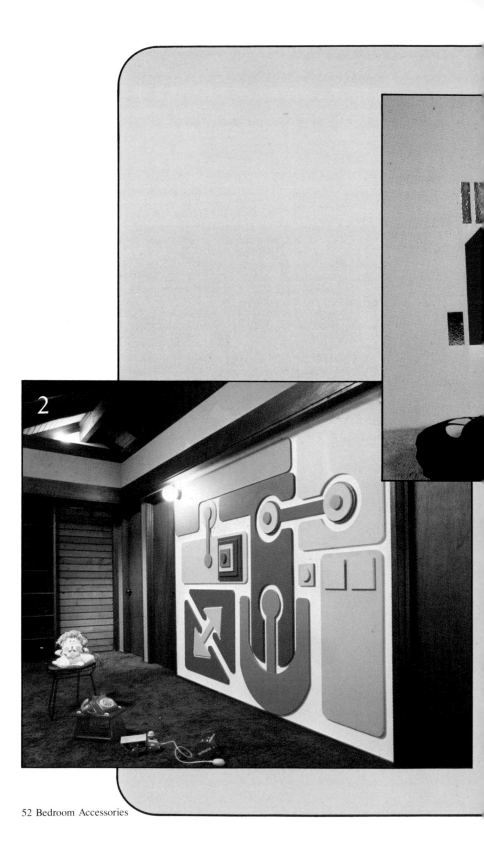

2 3-D MURAL: Let your imagination run wild with a wall of designs in plywood. Four sheets of ¾-inch plywood were used in this mural, but you could vary the thickness. Don't waste money on anything better than A-D, since one side won't show. First make a scale drawing of a design to fit your space, trace onto plywood, and cut with a jigsaw. Sand and paint the various pieces, then attach to wall with panel adhesive and finishing nails.

3 FIRETRUCK GRAPHIC: Create four alarm fun with this wall graphic made from self-adhesive plastic. Add a 48-inch-long wooden ladder, a running board shelf, a fabric "hose," and two floor pillows.

4

4 SUPER STAR MUSIC STAND: Inspire your budding instrumentalist with this star-motif music rack. Mount a 1½″ dowel to a star base cut from ¾″ particleboard. Cut the top star from tempered hardboard and attach a wood strip to hold the music. Slant the top of the dowel and fasten it to the bottom of the wood strip. Finally, paint the stand to suit the music maker.

5 INTERLOCK DESK/STORAGE: Accessible wall storage and a quiet study nook will assist your youngster achieve both good study habits and a sense of order. Built of pine, this efficient storage/study wall features a flip-up, fold-down study table in the center with plenty of storage for exercise equipment and even a file drawer. Plan #50353

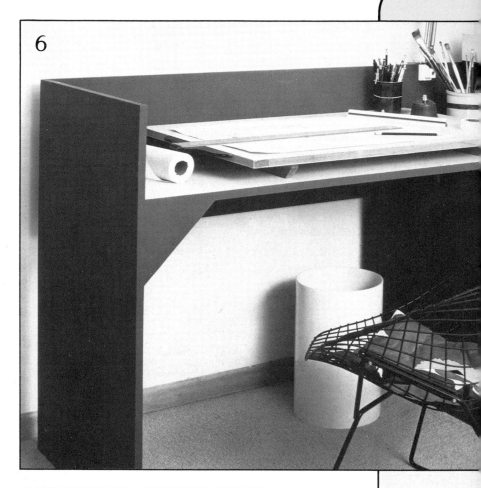

6 PLYWOOD STUDY DESK: All you
need for this simple desk are two sheets of fir plywood, nails, glue, and a covering for the top. Our
freestanding unit is $2'x5' \times 2\frac{1}{2}'$ to the desk top,
and an additional 6″ to the top of the back rail.
Begin by cutting a 36×24 piece for the end, two
30×24 pieces for the panels at right, one 12×60
piece for the back panel, one 23×60 piece for the
top, and three 18×24 pieces for the shelves. The
face piece above the shelves is 6×18 and is inserted between the two 30×24 panels. Note the
triangular gusset, added for stability. Its equal

sides are both 6". Assemble all of the pieces by nailing one to the other starting with the shelf box at right. Glue all joints before nailing; when finished, paint.

7 STAIRSTEP STORAGE: House youngsters' books, games, and other gear in easy-to-build cabinets with hinged doors. Install adjustable shelves to accommodate different collections as your children's interests change. These boxes rest on a 13" cantilevered platform.

8 HOBBY CENTER: Great for any room in the house, its doors and drawers conceal lots of clutter. Open shelves can display prized possessions. It's just the thing for a youngster's changing interests. Plan #50073

9 ADJUSTABLE DESK: Here's a desk that grows with the kids. The top is plastic laminate; movable blocks are made of $5/8''$ particleboard. Painted numerals tell the blocks' verticle dimensions. Plan #50315

10 SHOW-OFF STUDY CORNER: Cut six 80'' lengths of 2×2s for uprights and twelve $16^{1}/_{2}''$ 1×4s for crosspieces. Secure a 1×4 at the top and bottom of uprights and assemble each half of the unit as shown in the photo. Position another pair of crosspieces between each pair of uprights so tops of crosspieces measure $47^{1}/_{4}''$ from the floor. Cut 12 triangles from $3/4''$ plywood; secure at top and bottom. Notch remaining triangles and install adjustable shelving brackets. For desk surface, notch a $20 \times 42''$ piece of plywood and rest it on a pair of shelves. Sand all edges and surfaces; paint.

11 STORAGE UNIT: Your children will never be too grown up for this versatile wardrobe, chest of drawers, and shelf storage unit. It's made of three separate units, all stackable and interchangeable. Casters on the bottom make it easily transferable from room to room. Make it all of 3/4″ plywood using simple butt joints, finishing nails, and glue. Paint with enamel. Plan #50242

12 SHOW-OFF TOY STORAGE: With just 3 four-sided boxes, you can get a whole wall of storage for the kids. All the lumber is 1×12s with the front edges of all sides and shelves slightly rounded with sandpaper. Here the pink box is 26×48; the yellow is 18×75; the blue is 32×62. Build with butt joints, nail in the shelves you want to place permanently, then prime, paint and hang them on the wall with a ledger strip for each.

13

13 NURSERY ZOO: House all those stuffed animals in this $2 \times 4'$ cabinet, complete with cages for wild and woolly beasts. You'll need 24' of $1 \times 12''$ pine; $2 \times 4'$ of $1/8''$ hardboard; 9' of $1/4''$ wood dowels; two $10 \times 7^{3/4}''$ pieces of clear acrylic plastic; 4 brass hinge sets; nails; paint; 24' adhesive-backed metallic gold tape. From pine cut 2 end panels $24 \times 11^{1/4}''$; 1 top $48 \times 11^{1/4}''$; 2 shelves $46^{1/2} \times 11^{1/4}''$; 6 dividers $9^{1/4} \times 11^{1/4}''$; 1 toeboard $3^{1/4} \times 48''$.

Glue and nail sides to top, mitering corners. Glue and nail shelves spaced $9^{1/4}''$ apart. Glue and nail toeboard $2''$ in from bottom of front. Glue and nail $9^{1/4}''$ dividers spaced evenly across middle and bottom shelves. From the hardboard cut $20^{3/4} \times 48''$ back; glue and nail it to the top, middle and bottom shelves. Cut pine strips $3/4 \times 1^{1/8}''$ and length to fit 4 center openings. Construct door frames, mitering corners. Sand all pieces. Dado inside edges of 2 door frames. Insert acrylic into dados before gluing and nailing last side of each door frame in place. For bar doors, drill holes evenly spaced for 7 dowels in each door in top and bottom framing strips. Cut dowels to fit. Glue dowels in place. Glue and nail remaining sides of frames in place. Sand and paint frame and doors. Install hinges, door pulls, and magnetic catches. Apply adhesive-backed gold tape to front edges of unit.

14 CLOTHES RACK:

This kid-sized clothes rack is 36 × 36 with two 8″ shelves. You'll need 8′ of 1 × 8 clear pine; 4′ of 3/4″ dowel; 6′ of 2 × 2; and paint. Cut two 1 × 8 × 36 pieces and two 2 × 2 × 34½ pieces of pine. Cut the design on two 4 × 18 leg pieces and cut design on top support, 3″ wide by 4″ long. Notch bottom shelf for supports and assemble with nails and glue. Sand and paint.

15 KID-SIZE CLOTHING CENTER:

Build this "neat" project out of ½″ plywood, nailing a 26 × 75 back to a 26 × 15 bottom and adding a simple hamper box in front. Make the two cutouts for the caning, then paint the entire unit. Install the mirror, caning, hooks, hinge, and knob. Cut and paint the decorative molding; attach with brads.

Social Studies Activities

1. News map. Post a world map next to the television set to look up locales discussed in the news. Keep an atlas and an almanac nearby, too, to learn more about intriguing places.

2. Armchair travels. Take an imaginary trip around the world. Use a large (the bigger the better) map of the world to chart your tour route with a marker. Then use a marker of contrasting color to indicate your progress each day. Post the trip itinerary on the wall next to the map. Discuss local lore and customs of stops you made on each day of the trip.

3. Time line. Lay a roll of shelf paper or wrapping paper on the kitchen floor and chart history with a ruler and a marker. Children interested in American history, for example, will want to note such dates as 1776, 1865 and 1941. Then decorate the time line with drawings or photos clipped from magazines and newspapers and tape the chart to the wall.

4. Community map. A large piece of wrapping paper, a ruler or yardstick, and some marking pens are the ingredients for this map survey of the community. Locate and draw in major thoroughfares and familiar sights such as home, school, church, supermarket or park.

5. Current events board. Clip magazine and newspaper photos depicting news events and post the items on the board, changing them daily or weekly. Photos can be taped or pinned onto a bulletin board or to a piece of burlap or oilcloth.

6. Kid's calendar. Personalize a calendar — the bigger the better — by filling in the blanks with notes on the weather, trips, special activities, birthdays, and so on. Leave morning messages on the calendar, too — things to do today or just a "hello."

1 GIRLS' DOUBLE HEADBOARD:

During the day you can push one twin bed part way under this unit to get a few more square feet of floor space. Pillows go in the small cabinet under the lower shelf. Construction is simple. You just nail a few pieces of plywood to the 2 × 2 uprights. The canopy top is cut from fabric and glued on. Plan #50056

2 LOFTY BUNK: The fireman's pole makes getting out of bed a zip! Build the dresser and the

wall storage unit first, then install the box for the mattress and springs between them. Plan #50318

3 ACCOMMODATING ANGLES: Cutting across from door to window, the "upper level" offers space to sleep and study, and leaves the rest of the room wide open for dressing, play, and everything else. The platform is 14″ high, with 3 drawers built into the top riser. The design of the desk, window seat, and headboard are easily adapted to any room — just plan their sizes and locations around the window. Everything is plywood. Use a lower grade for the carpeted platform and a top grade for the built-ins so you can get the smooth, glossy finish. Plan #50319

4 HIGH RISE HABITAT: Built-ins can turn an ordinary bedroom into a multipurpose environment when they're planned as cleverly as this wall-to-wall system. The big idea is the 20″ platform that's built like a couple of giant plywood boxes. The bunk is a giant box also, supported by the wall and the extra storage closet. The 32″ deep desk bridges the space between closet and platform. And there's room for a pullout guest bunk below. Plan #50317

4 FOLD AWAY BED: Size the platform to any mattress you have. For a $39 \times 75''$ mattress, a $42 \times 78''$ piece of $3/4''$ plywood forms the bottom with a $3''$ edging on the top of all sides. Make the surround big enough to clear the bed by $1/4''$ at each end; plan $1''$ finger space along the top. Position the ledge — the piece on which the bed will pivot — approximately $10''$ above the floor, and recess the ledge $3/4''$ into the surround. Add a center divider, rails, and a $14\,1/2''$ rail in the middle. Use 2 pieces of $1/4''$ plywood for the back of the surround, butting horizontally behind the ledge.

Build the bed supports to fit in the two openings under the ledge. The supports pictured also double as storage bins, with $30 \times 9\,3/4''$ fronts. Make the storage bins shorter so they'll clear the middle rail. Inside dimensions of this unit are $6\,3/4 \times 20\,1/4 \times 7$. Use cutdown pieces of 2×8 for the ends nearest the middle of the bed so they can be drilled to accept heavy-duty casters. Nail small spacers to the backs of the bins to keep them from closing too far. Mount the bins with hinges. Install the bed platform in the opening by mounting a piano hinge — first to the back edge of the bed, then to the ledge. (The bed, when closed, will be flush with the sides of the surround.) Use $1/2''$ dowels to hold the bed closed, inserting them into holes drilled down through the top of the surround into the bed frame. Nail stops to the inside of the surround on each side to keep the bed from closing past center. Add a simple box shelf above — or otherwise adapt the unit to your storage needs.

5 BUCKBOARD BED: Build your little wrangler this bouncy Western bed with its wagon wheels and buckboard seat. The frame is 1×8 pine, with 2×4 legs, and accommodates 66×30 box spring and mattress. Plan #50241

6 TWIN BUNKS: This unusual bunk bed is not only attractive but great for kids, because it has a catchall storage space in one end. Both bunks are designed for box springs and mattresses, but you could use foam mattresses alone for younger children. You build these bunks in three different sections in your shop, then assemble them in the bedroom. This kind of construction makes moving easy, too. A really practical answer for two kids sharing a room. Plan #50113

7 SPACE SAVER BUNKS: You get a lot in a little space with this bunk bed. Besides beds for two children there's a sliding door closet plus two drawers for clothing or toys. Foam mattresses on the bunks are easy to fit in and good for young backs. You build the bunks in component parts, then fasten them together. If you can build plywood boxes, this project is a snap. Plan #50096

5

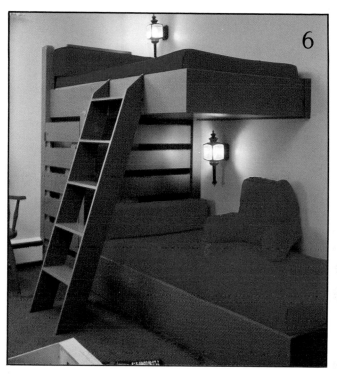

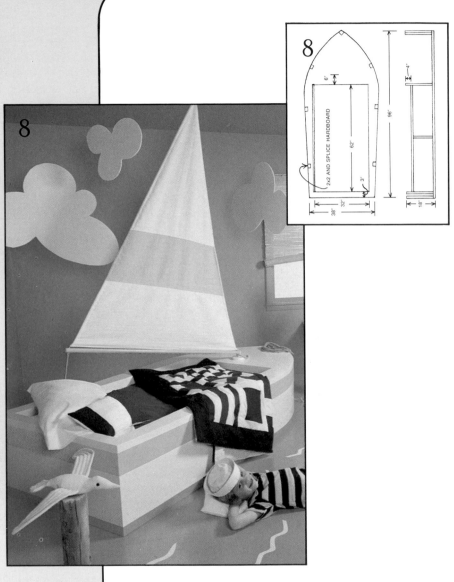

8 SHIP BED: To form this seaworthy bed's frame, connect the top and bottom sections with 18″ long 1×2s. Position your cutout piece 4″ below the deck on a support made from scrap ³/4″ lumber and ³/4″ plywood. This is your recessed mattress platform. Cut two 8′ long × 19″ wide hardboard strips. Starting at the bow, glue and nail

the hardboard to the top and bottom, ending on a 2×2 support. Fill the remaining area with hardboard. The mast and sail support is nylon rope tied to screw eyes in the deck and ceiling, then run from the ceiling to the closet pole boom. Make the sail of crinkle cloth, cut and sewn to fit the outline created by the rope and boom. Then, sand, prime, and paint.

9 BEDMOBILE: What child wouldn't welcome this colorful bedmobile, fully equipped with built-in desk and closet? The bed can be assembled in pieces, then put together to make a complete unit. Plan #50392

10 STURDY STORAGE BUNK: Let the dimensions of your bunk-bed-sized mattress determine the size of this 56″ high unit. From ¾″ plywood, cut 3 uprights, the doors, shelves, and a deck to support the mattress. Position uprights, and support the deck with 1×3 cleats nailed to the wall. Cut and secure the back of the shelf area and the 1×8 mattress surround. Attach a ladder made from 1×3s and dowels. Hang the doors, add shelves, and paint. Add vinyl tape stripes.

11 STORAGE BED: For this storage bed mark pieces for $72 \times 30\frac{1}{2} \times 17\frac{1}{2}″$ box. On front, center a $40\frac{1}{2} \times 15\frac{3}{4}″$ opening. Mark $14\frac{1}{2} \times 12\frac{1}{2}″$ cutouts for side drawers. Cut box pieces and rectangles from front. Construct box, lining the opening with plywood; glue and nail 1×3s on edge around top. Build a $40 \times 28\frac{1}{2}″$ platform from plywood; edge with 1×3s. Add casters, hinge opening cover; sand and paint.

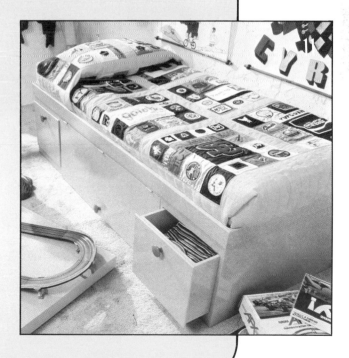

12 PLAYHOUSE/BUNK: In this versatile project an extra-long single mattress was used to allow enough width for play space beneath. The structure is supported by the ready-to-finish dresser units in front and by 4 × 4s at the other corners. The sides of the platform itself are made of ³/₄″ plywood. Construct the guardrail of a 1 × 4 mounted to 2 shelf supports attached to the 1 × 6 frame and the plywood base. Make the ladder of 1 × 4s, adjusting the slope to the space available.

13 ROOM DIVIDER: Solve the privacy problem of a shared bedroom with this study/storage divider. There are separate wardrobes, dual desks, shelves and cupboards. Plan #50050

13

14 PLATFORM BED: This practical bed-storage unit is a good example of double-duty furniture. It consists of a 6′ × 39″ slab of 3/4″ plywood, a twin mattress, and 3 drawers which are 14″ × 8″. The cases for the drawers, and the bases, are 29″ deep. You can plan the drawers that deep if you have the room to pull them all the way out for access. If you have space on both sides of the bed, you may want to build another set that would pull out from the other side.

15 BUNK BED STORAGE: Substitute storage for an unused upper bunk by using 44′ of rough 1 × 4s to construct a "cage" of horizontal and vertical boards over the top bunk. Determine the size of your finished storage area by adjusting the height of your 1 × 4s. Along the front, attach 3 window shades, mounting them to the top 1 × 4, and add one shade to the end of the bed.

16 SHARED SPACE BUNK: If you have two children who must share one small bedroom, you know the problems it can create. This plan offers separate sleeping, study, and storage zones for each child — plus adequate open floor space. The plan is suitable for a 9 × 12 or 12 × 12 room. Plan #50102

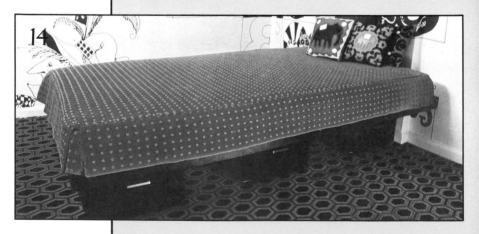

17 PERSONAL HEADBOARD: Cut out 16″ high letters from plywood or hardboard and a base to fit the width of the bed. Pad and cover each letter with 1″ foam and fabric for this very special, personalized headboard.

18 HEARTFELT PROJECTS: This junior bed adapts to the size of the mattress, so just add 3″ to the length and width then cut a piece of ³/4″ plywood to these dimensions. Join lengths of 1″ pine to create headboard, footboard and sides. Headboard is 20″ high; footboard is 13″ high; sides are 11″ high. Contour the footboard and headboard as shown. Cut a heart-shaped motif in each. Cut an area in each side piece for easier access. Glue and nail plywood bottom inside frame so that top of plywood is recessed 7³/4″ from top of sides. Glue and screw 2 × 2 legs to inside corners so that top of sides are 18¹/2″ from the floor. Sand; finish as desired.

For the rocker follow the diagram, cutting pieces from 1″ pine laminate. The seat is 13 × 14″ and the back is 13 × 15″. Heart hooks are made of the cutouts from the rocker and bed with 1″ dowels inserted as pegs.

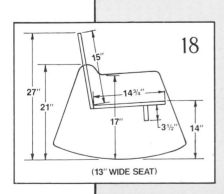

15"

14³/₄"

27"

21"

17"

3¹/₂"

14"

(13" WIDE SEAT)

18

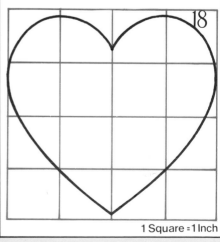

18

1 Square = 1 Inch

19 BUNKS AND MORE: The modular feeling of this bunk bed plus its companion wall of built-ins is easily adapted to most bedrooms and many styles of homes. Plan #50225

20 TOTAL ROOM PLAN: This single bed plus its wall of storage and study components help to organize lots of clutter and still provide plenty of functional space. Plan #50224

21 BUNK WITH BONUSES: More than just a bunk bed, this unit also boasts a desk, shelf, and storage bins. The main ingredients of this sturdy unit are plywood and dimension pine lumber, plus $1/4 \times 2''$ lag screws. Plan #50397

21

22 SPACE-SAVER UNITS: Solve several space problems with this set of built-ins which includes a desk, closet and toy shelves. Although they are shown built along the same wall, they can be placed around the room for a more convenient arrangement. Plan #50273

23 STUDY/SLEEP CENTER: This built-in is more than just a bunk; there's room for a guest, a study desk, and a playhouse. The unit is 4' high and 6½' long in each direction. It's built of ¾" plywood with a 2 × 2 vertical for stability. Plan #50264

24 FREE-FORM WALL UNIT: Designed to fill an awkwardly high space, you can adapt the idea to fit any wall you have. It's basically a ¾" plywood base on which are mounted boxes of various sizes and shapes to accommodate the changing paraphernalia of a child from birth to young adult. The desk is an ammunition box from a surplus store with wood knobs and a chain attached. A ¼" dowel runs through the sides to hold up books and magazines.

RAINY DAY ACTIVITIES

1. Paper houses. Sift through newspapers and magazines for pictures of furniture that belong in different rooms of the house. Then divide a large newspaper sheet into sections labeled living room, bedroom, dining room, and so on. Paste in pictures of the furniture that fits into different rooms.

2. Read and do. Everybody gets a written list of ten things to read and do. For example: gather up a stack of newspapers, fold them three times, and tie the bundle with a string. Tasks can be far-fetched or practical chores that need doing around the house.

3. Sense boxes. For a taste box, include small containers of vinegar, salt, and sugar; for a touch box, cotton, a stone, a piece of smooth glass (without sharp edges), and sandpaper; and for a smell box, an assortment of kitchen condiments and spices. Then blindfold children before they guess the contents of each box.

4. Alphabet olympics. Print capital letters on twenty-six index cards and small letters on another set of twenty-six cards. Then put the scrambled letters in order, read the letters aloud, and name words that start with the letters. Start with small groups of letters and work up to all twenty-six.

5. Kitchen alphabet hunt. Find letters of the alphabet around the kitchen — on soup cans, cereal boxes, and such. Track down five A's, or three C's, or any number of combinations of letters. Start with easy-to-find letters and work up to more difficult ones.

6. Hypothesizing. At the kitchen sink, line up some bar soap, a dry sock, a full plastic bottle of shampoo, a wet sponge, a dry sponge, an empty bottle and other objects. Hypothesize beforehand which of the objects will float or sink, then test the hypotheses.

1 BUCKET NIGHTSTAND: High-impact plastic buckets are among the sturdiest totes you can find. Here, two bright blue window washer buckets (available at cleaning supply outlets) are nested in a ³/₄″ flakeboard shelf to create a quick and easy nightstand. Using the dimensions of the buckets as a guide, cut the pieces for the shelves. Miter the uprights and the top, and cut dadoes, along the uprights to receive the center shelf and bottom. Fill the area beneath the bottom shelf with a 1 × 2. Sand, prime, and paint.

2 MINIATURE FURNITURE: Suit a child's imaginative world with a roomful of child-size furniture. Our china cabinet, chairs, tables, and love seat are projects for you to build for that

very special gift. Plan packet includes large, professional drawings, materials list, woodcutting diagrams, and easy-to-follow instructions.
Plan #50398

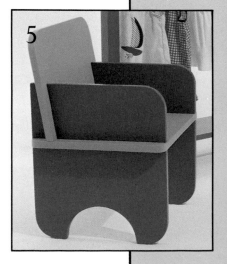

3 FIT-TOGETHER FURNITURE: Kids love turn-about and this booth turns into a table and two benches when flipped over. Flip it back down again, tuck the seats in once more, and the entire unit is easily transportable. All you'll need is one 4×8 sheet of $1/2''$ plywood, glue, nails, and paint. The project's butt-joint construction makes it a snap to build. It measures $30 \times 20 \times 18^{1}/_{2}''$ and will take lots of wear and tear. Plan #50312

4 FOLD-UP WALL UNIT: You'll get plenty of display space and a desk to boot from one plywood sheet. The cutouts form both shelves and supports. Cut the wood, then reattach pieces with continuous hinges, and mount it to the wall. Plan #50366

5 SLIP-TOGETHER CHAIR: Make this notched chair of just 4 pieces cut from $1/2$ sheet of $3/4''$ particleboard. Cut the seat $16^{1}/_{2} \times 15''$ and measure $1^{1}/_{4}''$ in from either side for notches, $13/16''$ wide and $7^{1}/_{2}$ deep. Round off opposite corners with $1^{1}/_{4}''$ radius. Cut 2 sides $15 \times 17^{1}/_{2}''$ high then round off 3 edges with $1^{1}/_{4}''$ radius. At squared corner, measure in $2''$ for chair back slot. Make slot $13/16''$ wide and $3''$ deep at a 10 degree angle. For seat slot measure down $6''$ from top, and cut $13/16''$ wide slot $7^{1}/_{2}''$ deep. Cut out $4''$ radius at base. Cut back $16^{1}/_{2} \times 12''$. Make notches $1^{1}/_{4}''$ in from each side, $6''$ deep. Round opposite corners with $1^{1}/_{4}''$ radius, sand and paint. Slip together.

6 EASY FURNITURE: Three sheets of 3/4″ fir plywood make our modular table, chairs and shelves. Chairs are four 12″ cubes. Six 12 × 12 × 24 rectangles form the table and window shelf base. The remaining wood serves as tabletop and wall shelves. Just glue and nail the boxes, then sand, paint and stack.

7 CUBE FURNITURE: For one table and one chair you'll need 4 × 8′ of 1″ thick particleboard. Using the diagram construct table as a 5-sided cube with glued and nailed butt joints at the sides and top. Construct the back and seat of the chair, set them between sides with 1 × 1 × 1″ strips underneath. Set top back and lower front panels flush with side edges. Add back last.

15″

15″

15″

7

TABLE

10″

14″

11″

11″

14″

13″

24″

24″

24″

CHAIR

7

8 SIDE-STEP ROCKER: What could be handier for the young ones around the house? A rocker is on one side, a step platform on the other, and the unit can be built in an evening. Use $3/4''$ plywood throughout. Adapt the dimensions to your needs, but keep the unit wide enough so it won't tip easily. Make step risers and treads at least $8''$ deep. Lay out the step design on the sidepieces before gluing and nailing them together. Seal, sand and finish with epoxy paint for long life.

9 THEATER CHAIR: Built from 1 sheet $1/2''$ AB fir plywood and two $17 \times 1 \times 2''$ pieces of lumber, this chair/puppet theater is sure to be a main attraction. Cut three $2 \times 3'$ pieces rounding outside corners on 2. Cut $12 \times 15''$ window in each. Glue and nail sides to front with side windows at top and front window at bottom. Glue and nail 1×2s to each side, $21''$ below top and flush with window. Add an $18 \times 23''$ seat.

10 HEART SEATS: This child-sized gossip bench is perfect for a heart-to-heart talk. Each occupant has a separate — but equal — space. Plan #50452

11 CHILD'S CHAIR:

11 CHILD'S CHAIR: Your toddler will love this animal-faced chair, and you'll appreciate its sure-footed sturdiness. You'll need 28″ of 1 × 10″ pine and 20″ of 1 × 12″ pine. Using the pattern, cut the seat, back and sides. Sand and assemble the pieces using nails and glue. Paint the chair yellow. When dry, transfer facial details to the back and paint.

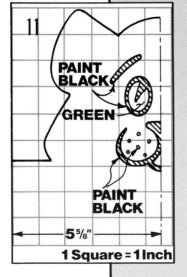

11

PAINT BLACK

GREEN

PAINT BLACK

5⅝″

1 Square = 1 Inch

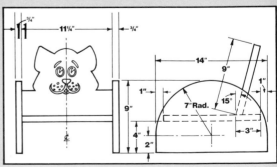

11 | ¾″ | 11¼″ | ¾″ | 14″ | 9″ | 1″ | 1″ | 9″ | 7″ Rad. | 15° | 4″ | 2″ | 3″

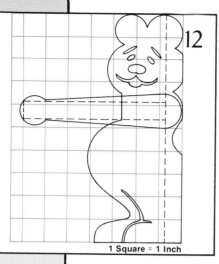

1 Square = 1 Inch

12 BEAR RACK: For this appealing child's coat rack use $^3/_4''$ pine for the 6 × 24″ shelf and $^1/_2''$ plywood for the bears and the backing, plus $^1/_2''$ dowels for the pegs. Cut two bears following the pattern, a 24 × 8″ backing piece, and a 6 × 24″ shelf. Glue and nail backing to bears; position shelf between bears' arms and secure in place. Sand and paint as desired.

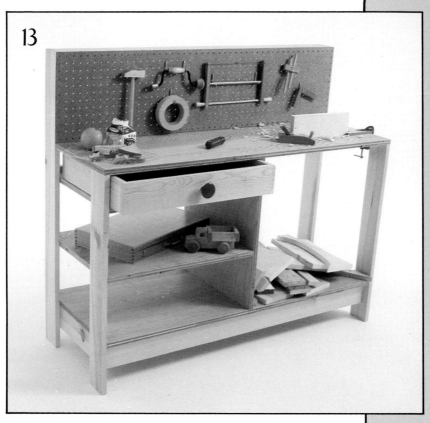

13

14

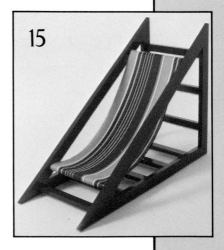

15

13 WORKBENCH: Start this child-size workbench by cutting two 29¼″ front legs and two 42″ back legs from 1 × 4s. Cut two 46½″ and two 14½″ pieces from 1 × 4s for bottom bracing and a 46½″ header to span the back legs at the top. From ¾″ AD plywood, cut 18 × 48″ work surface, lower shelves and dividers. Build a drawer from 1 × 4s and insert a hardboard bottom in ¼″ deep dadoes cut along lower sides. Assemble and add pegboard along the top. Brace the panel with a 1 × 1 stop, nailed to the work surface, and center a vertical 1 × 4 divider behind the panel.

14 TOY-BEARING TREE: There's perching space galore for bushels of toys and collectibles on this delightful storage tree. Apple cutouts serve as hooks for hanging lightweight items, and eight shelves hold toys and games when not in use. Cut the pieces from flakeboard and slip-joint them together, using base and shelves as braces. Add a coat of paint and apply a contrasting color to the apple cutouts.

15 FLIP CHAIR: Build the sides and braces of this flip chair from 3″ wide 1¼″ lumber. Cut two 36″ uprights and two 51″ base pieces. Using half-lap joints, glue and screw uprights to base pieces. Cut two lengths equal to the distance between the top of the uprights and the tip of the base and angle the ends. Secure to the uprights and base with half-lap joints to form the triangle. From 2″ strips of 1¼″ lumber, cut eight 20½″ cross braces, 3 along uprights and 5 along base. Inset 1″ dowel 12″ from each pointed end. Sand frame and paint with high-gloss enamel. Cut a 16″ wide fabric sling. Fold around dowels and sew securely.

16 PLAY TABLE: Painting is lots more fun when there's another artist at work. When painting temporarily loses its intrigue, the easel folds down to make a big flat table top complete with a roomy storage shelf underneath for all sorts of toys.
Plan #50034

17 JUNIOR FURNITURE: These pint-sized pieces of furniture are built from rugged ¾" plywood to hold up under the rowdiest tea party. The table has a plastic laminate top, so crayon marks or spills wipe off with a damp cloth.
Plan #50126

OUTDOOR PLAY

OUTDOOR ACTIVITIES

1. Disappearing signs. All you need are a warm, sunny day, a driveway or sidewalk, a pail of water, and a couple of big brushes. This writing activity is fun, helps develop muscle control, and doesn't leave any permanent graffiti. Write messages, or names, or whatever comes to mind and watch them disappear because of the evaporation, which also gives you an opportunity to explain a science concept.

2. Disappearing water. Put some water in a dish in a sunny spot. Mark the water level on the dish. Then place another dish with an equal amount of water in a shady place and mark the water level on it. Observe what happens each day.

3. Thermometer fun. Use whatever indoor and outdoor thermometers you have around the house. What temperature is it in the room? What temperature is it on the patio, under a tree, out on the sidewalk? What happens when you put the thermometer in the refrigerator?

4. Weighing in. Bring the bathroom scales out onto the patio or porch and start weighing — anything and everything. See how much the puppy or kitten weighs if it will hold still. Fill pails from the sandpile. Begin by venturing guesses about what different things weigh, and then weigh them. The children might want to take turns guessing each others' weight.

5. Light entertainment. Have the children stand within a shaded area such as under a tree or an eave, then extend their hands into the sunlit area. Make the simple animal shapes such as rabbits or ducks by adjusting the fingers and then just let them use their imaginations to see what they can create. Encourage them to invent stories or use two characters with dialogue.

1 CLIMBER'S DELIGHT: The blue and green panels of the mini-high-rise are interchangeable; screw them to the outside or just lay them in as flooring. Notched corners prevent slipping. For materials you'll need 4 × 4s, ³/₄" plywood, wood screws and paint. Plan #50175

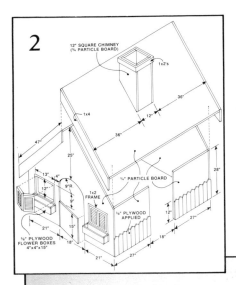

2

12" SQUARE CHIMNEY
(¾" PARTICLE BOARD)

1x2's

36"

1x4

12"

36"

47"

25"

¾" PARTICLE BOARD

28"

13"

4"

9" R.

12"

9"

1x2
FRAME

¾" PLYWOOD
APPLIED

12"

27"

15"

9"

¾" PLYWOOD
FLOWER BOXES
4"x4"x15"

21"

18"

18"

21"

27"

2

2 QUILTED PLAYHOUSE: Here's a delightful kid-sized cottage that's a beauty to behold, and its flakeboard shell is designed for easy building and moving. Quilt batting is glued to the shell with a layer of calico tacked on top. Each padded shingle is stitched separately, then stapled in place. Uncovered surfaces are painted with enamel. If you prefer an exclusively outdoor playhouse, just substitute exterior-grade plywood. Plan #50388

3 OUTDOOR DRAMA: A playhouse, a stage, and a castle all rolled into one, this structure consists of exterior grade plywood over a 2 × 3 framework. The side draperies can be let down to act as stage curtains. Plan #50464

4 CASTLE PLAYHOUSE: Will the brave knight vanquish the fiery dragon and rescue the fair damsel? We don't know, but we do know you can fit this six-piece particleboard playhouse together faster than you can lower the drawbridge. Plan #50404

5 PLAY GYM: This miniature gym lets kids climb one side, slide down the other, then tunnel through the center. Plan #50446

6 IGLOO PLAYHOUSE: This novel 5 × 4 × 2½′ play structure is constructed of ¾″ exterior plywood cut into three 48 × 30″ arcs. The front arc features 2 adjacent 20 × 18″ arcs, one of which opens into an 18″ tunnel. The arcs are joined by pieces of 1″ lumber cut to 36″ lengths, with the tunnel employing 24″ lengths. Plan #50394

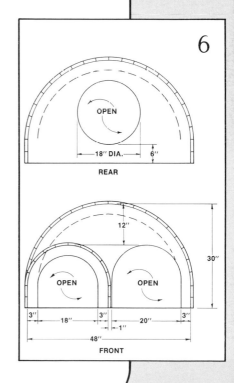

7

8

7 PLAYHOUSE: Fun never stops in this multi-level playhouse with its four separate levels. Children never tire of exploring the various entries, decks and ladders. The playhouse is basically an 8' cube made from 11$\frac{1}{2}$ sheets of 4 × 8-foot $\frac{3}{4}''$ plywood. Plan #50191

8 ELEVATED HIDEAWAY: Maybe you can talk the kids into sharing this tree-top screened house. This 10 × 16' room will give them hours of enjoyment with plenty of protection from both bugs and falls. Plan #50239

9 CONTEMPORARY PLAY UNIT:
Hours of climbing, twisting and crawling fun are packed into this bright backyard mini-mountain. You'll need three $30 \times 60''$ panels of $3/4''$ exterior grade plywood plus two $30 \times 30''$ panels. Cut the $18''$ diameter holes and the diagonal as shown. Assemble the unit with 2×4 posts — for maximum stability sink $8'$ long 2×4s into the ground. You may want to build it of $24 \times 48''$ panel for little tots or big $4 \times 8'$ panels for larger kids.

10 WATCHTOWER PLAYHOUSE: It looks like a mountain fire-watch tower, but this rugged structure is really a combination play loft and storage area. A ladder at the far end leads to the loft, which is sheltered by a plywood roof. Below, there's a lockable storage compartment for your tools and outdoor accessories. Plan #50192

11 ALL-AROUND PLAY UNIT: This treated pine set combines a treeless treehouse, swings, and a jungle gym. Six old tires positioned under the lower deck provide a safe obstacle course. With this in your backyard, you'll be quite popular with the "swing set" on your block. Plan #50465

12

12 SAND OR SPLASH: Assemble this $4 \times 6'$ deck by nailing 1×4s atop a framework of 1×6s. Four 1×8s and a $1/2''$ plywood bottom form the $2^{1}/_{2} \times 3'$ sandbox. Or build a circular frame and slip-in a plastic wading pool. You'll eliminate the mud hole and add hours of pleasure for the kids.

12

13 PLAY STRUCTURE: Besides being a real treat for the kids, this play unit can go with you when you move. It's made from five components that you build beforehand, then assemble with lag bolts. (This one went up in six hours.) All platforms are $4 \times 4'$ squares of $5/8''$ plywood over 2×4 framing. Posts are 4×4s resting on concrete piers. Plan #50262

14 PLAY AND STORE: With sand below ensuring soft landings, who wouldn't pick the ramp exit from this combination playhouse/storage shed? There's a ladder on the other side, but that's only good for going up. The lower level houses mundane things like tools, lawnmowers and bikes. Plan #50240

15 PLAYHOUSE/STORAGE: This miniature house will please any youngsters and give them a place of their own. Maybe they'll even invite you over for milk and cookies. Built of exterior grade plywood with a corrugated roof, this simple playhouse also has room for the adults' lawn and garden equipment. Plan #50147

16 SANDBOX/STORAGE: Here's proof that a storage shed doesn't have to look like a storage shed. The three stairstep modules — 32" square — are 16, 32 and 48 inches high, the latter two interconnecting to accommodate a mower. Materials include three 4×8 sheets of 3/4" exterior plywood, a few pieces of dimension lumber, some hasps, hinges and paint. Plan #50313

17 A-FRAME PLAYHOUSE: Make this multi-level adventure world from plywood and standard grade lumber. Use sturdy posts for support and rope for the ladder. From sandbox to tree-high second story, this place is perfect for kids. Plan #50087

18 A-FRAME PLAY UNIT: Keep your youngster out of the trees by building this elevated A-frame. It begins as 6 posts, an elongated cross-piece, and some bracing. The swings are just chains and strips of canvas. Later, add the tree house and ladder, and finally, the basketball backboard and court. Treated redwood will last several childhoods with minimal maintenance. Plan #50178

19 BALCONY STORAGE SHED: This sturdy $6 \times 12'$ jungle gym is as rugged as any Little Leaguer. While kids climb its railed frame, enclosed inside is a storage shed where you can stash garden equipment and the like. Remaining open area could house a sandbox or a bike port. Basic framework is made from $4 \times 4''$ posts and 2×4s. Walls are $3/4''$ plywood. Plan #50141

20 PLAY AREA: If there's no room left for expanding the children's play area, look up. There's plenty of space overhead for some of the best fun of all. This post-and-beam-framed haven with several swings, a basketball goal, a big tree house, chinning bar and gym will keep them all happy. Set the 4×4 posts in concrete for extra strength and sandwich the upper framing beams around the posts. Nail 2×4s to posts to support

the exterior grade plywood floor of the house. In-set panels of perforated hardboard to form the half-wall of the "dwelling" and paint bright colors. Use galvanized pipe for long spans of monkey bars and ladder rungs. Mount basketball backboard, hang the big swing, and step back fast to avoid the stampede of neighborhood kids.
Plan #50153

21

21 PLAYHOUSE: Tarzan never had it so good. Ladder access to the 8 × 10' house and rope swings for quick exits make this structure extremely adaptable. The roof beam extends 8' beyond the house to support the 2 fire swings that double as climbing ropes. Sand beneath the swings cushions falls and provides building material for castles and racetracks for toy cars. Plan #50336

22 NAUTICAL PLAYHOUSE: Anchors aweigh! The S.S. Playtime is ready to set sail for distant ports. With their very own flag topping the mast, a sturdy deck railing for safety and plywood cabin, they're ready for hours of adventuresome fun. Plan #50138

23 COTTAGE PLAYHOUSE: Build this little garden cottage for your youngsters' home-away-from- home. You just nail together a stack of 2 × 4 frame members, then fasten them to the 2 × 4 and plywood floor. Add the plywood deck, then cover the whole house with hardboard siding. Paint batten strips for the roof and nail them on, too. Set a ready-made awning window in the roof. Plan #50139.

The Garlinghouse Company is pleased to re-issue these Better Homes and Gardens project plans. It is our hope that this publication will assist you in making your home both more efficient and more enjoyable.

1. ORDERS should include full payment.

2. CHECKS AND MONEY ORDERS should be made payable to: The Garlinghouse Company.

3. MASTERCARD AND VISA CREDIT CARDS may be used for orders of $20.00 or more. Be sure to include your credit card number, the expiration date and your signature. We cannot process your order without this information.

4. COST OF PLANS is $4.95 for any plan ordered.

5. SHIPPING AND HANDLING CHARGES are $1.75 for the first plan that you order and $.50 for each plan thereafter.

6. MAIL ORDERS TO:
Garlinghouse/BH&G Project Plans,
P.O. Box 10251,
Des Moines, IA 50336

7. CANADIAN ORDERS should include payment in U.S. currency.

Ship To: **Payment:** ☐ Check or Money Order
Name _____ ☐ MasterCard ☐ Visa
Street _____ Apt. No. _____ Card No. _____
City _____ State _____ Zip _____ Exp. Date _____ **No C.O.D. Orders**
Signature _____

Item No.	Description	Qnty.	Total	Shipping & Handling	Total

Garlinghouse/BH&G Project Plans G11 Order Total _____
P.O. Box 10251 Iowa/Kansas Residents Add 4% Sales Tax _____
Des Moines, IA 50336 Total _____

Ship To: **Payment:** ☐ Check or Money Order
Name _____ ☐ MasterCard ☐ Visa
Street _____ Apt. No. _____ Card No. _____
City _____ State _____ Zip _____ Exp. Date _____ **No C.O.D. Orders**
Signature _____

Item No.	Description	Qnty.	Total	Shipping & Handling	Total

Garlinghouse/BH&G Project Plans G11 Order Total _____
P.O. Box 10251 Iowa/Kansas Residents Add 4% Sales Tax _____
Des Moines, IA 50336 Total _____

Ship To: **Payment:** ☐ Check or Money Order
Name _____ ☐ MasterCard ☐ Visa
Street _____ Apt. No. _____ Card No. _____
City _____ State _____ Zip _____ Exp. Date _____ **No C.O.D. Orders**
Signature _____

Item No.	Description	Qnty.	Total	Shipping & Handling	Total

Garlinghouse/BH&G Project Plans G11 Order Total _____
P.O. Box 10251 Iowa/Kansas Residents Add 4% Sales Tax _____
Des Moines, IA 50336 Total _____